RIO THE RACCOON

Rio the raccoon was all alone,
in the forest far from home.

He felt sad in his heart and
scared in his chest.

His mind would not settle.
His body could not rest.

It was dark and cold, with no one about.
So, Rio's mind filled up with doubt.

He had never been alone before and to get back home, he'd need to explore.

Even though his eyes were streaming tears, Rio started his journey to conquer his fears.

Rio saw the sun begin to rise and much to his surprise, he saw creatures all around - a family of finches, ants on the ground.

Rio followed the ants, which led to a tree. He started somewhere and that is the key.

Inside the tree lived an owl so wise,
with coffee brown feathers, and bright yellow eyes.

Rio approached her and said "I'm lost."
She said, "I'll help, but it will come at a cost.

You must leave behind your fear to fail.
Learn to adapt and you will prevail."

Rio agreed and went on his way.
He walked and walked, but to his dismay
the path he was following had disappeared.
And all of a sudden Rio felt weird.

His heart began pounding, his stomach a-rumble.
He almost gave up 'til he heard a faint mumble.

Rio looked to his feet and locked eyes with a snake -
all coiled up, with scales opaque.

Rio asked, "What did you say?"
The snake replied, "I can show you the way."

The snake became Rio's good friend,
someone on whom he could depend.

One true friend is all you need, someone who likes to see you succeed.

When Rio's jump across the river fell short, Snake was there to show his support.

And when Rio was sad, or anxious or scared,
his friend Snake was quick to show Rio he cared.

Friends can come in all shapes and sizes.
They are there for you when trouble arises.

From forest to river, to a nicely paved road,
Snake took Rio to meet Mr. Toad.

With this new and thoughtful information,
Rio made time for meditation.

He closed his eyes and breathed in deep.
Each deep breath brought him closer to sleep.

Rio awoke feeling calm and prepared.
With his friends by his side, he was much less scared.

When Rio felt fear or when he was in doubt,
he trusted himself to figure it out.

Rio improved his self-esteem,
then he set a goal to follow his dream.

He bid Snake and Mr. Toad a grateful farewell, and began walking towards a very sweet smell.

Then Rio heard a buzzing sound and
saw some honey bees flying around.

He followed the honey bees back to their hive and
asked their Queen, "How do you thrive?"

The Queen replied with just three rules.
She said to Rio, "Remember these tools.

When you start to lose all hope, there are positive ways that you can cope.

Staying calm in the face of stress is necessary to achieve success.

Do not become disconnected, and your life will unfold better than expected."

The Queen pointed Rio in the right direction and on his way he found time for reflection.

He realized that from the moment of birth, within each creature is an inherent worth.

And with each experience and lesson learned, a full and meaningful life is earned.

His journey helped him to learn and grow and to become aware of what he did not know.

His new perspective allowed Rio to see that he was exactly where he needed to be.

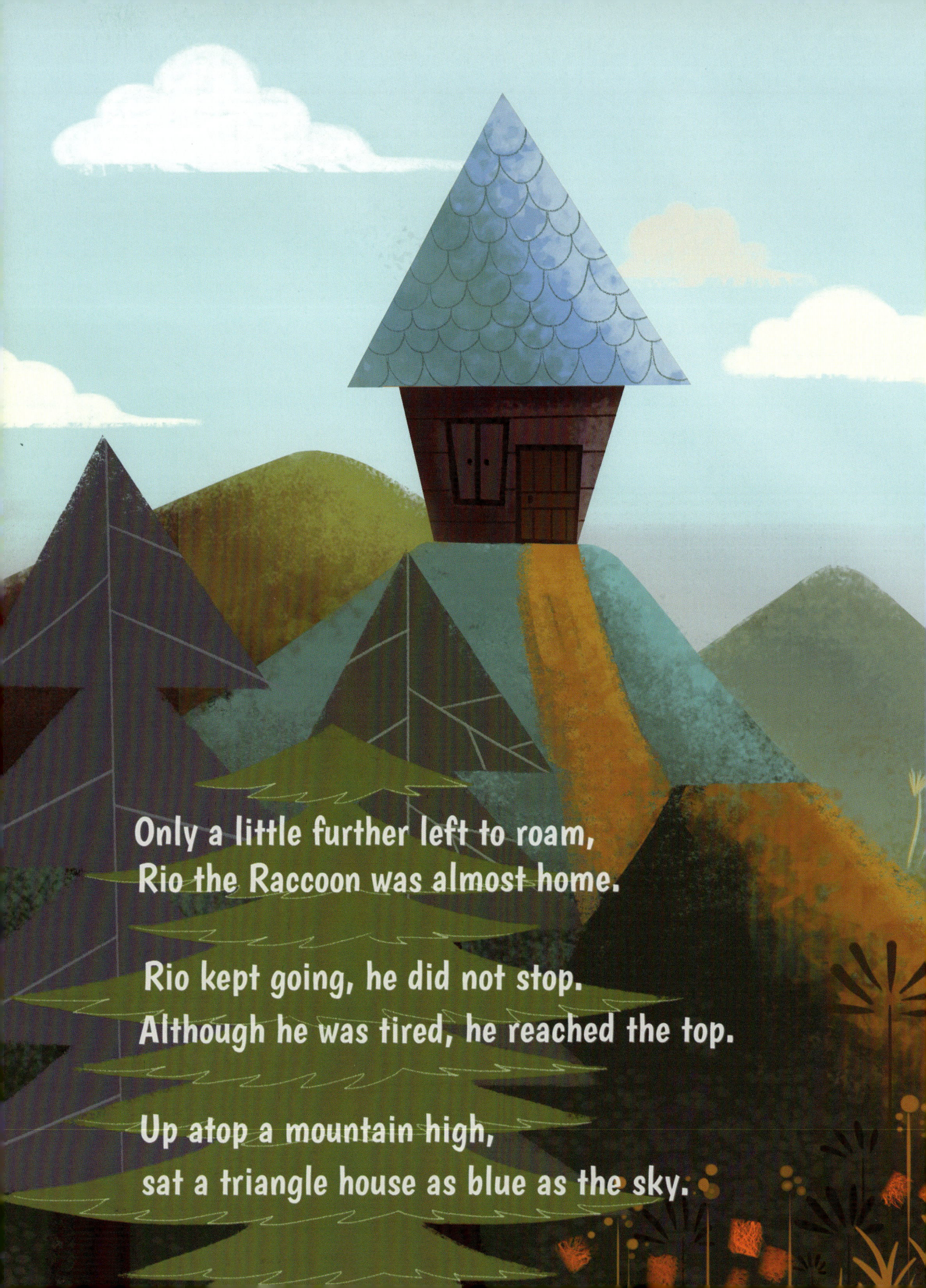
Only a little further left to roam,
Rio the Raccoon was almost home.

Rio kept going, he did not stop.
Although he was tired, he reached the top.

Up atop a mountain high,
sat a triangle house as blue as the sky.

Rio explained that on his journey alone, he became quite comfortable with the unknown.

He then taught his sister a powerful notion: Breathing through feeling to control her emotions.

Now Rio is equipped to help others heal because he is in charge of the way that he feels.

Rio is creative, courageous and strong.
He had been that way all along.

Rio is capable, smart and kind, with a heart full of love and an intelligent mind.

You can be Rio, resilient and ready to follow your dreams, confident and steady.

You must not fear failure or accept defeat.
You must learn from mistakes and do not repeat.

Have faith in yourself, you are destined for greatness.
The journey is windy, do not expect straightness.

Life is a river, constantly flowing.
Now go on your way, you've got to keep growing.